Written by Loris Lesynski   Illustrated by Gerry Rasmussen

CRAZY ABOUT BASKETBALL!

annick press
Toronto • Vancouver • New York

For writer
Claire Mackay,
who loves words
beyond words

LL

© 2013 Loris Lesynski (text)
© 2013 Gerry Rasmussen (illustrations)
Design & Art Direction by Loris Lesynski, Laugh Lines Design

Annick Press Ltd.

We acknowledge the support of the Canada Council for the Arts,
the Ontario Arts Council, and the Government of Canada through
the Canada Book Fund (CBF) for our publishing activities.

ONTARIO ARTS COUNCIL
CONSEIL DES ARTS DE L'ONTARIO
50 YEARS OF ONTARIO GOVERNMENT SUPPORT OF THE ARTS
50 ANS DE SOUTIEN DU GOUVERNEMENT DE L'ONTARIO AUX ARTS

Cataloging in Publication
Lesynski, Loris
    Crazy about basketball! / by Loris Lesynski ; illustrated by Gerry Rasmussen.

ISBN 978-1-55451-541-7 (bound).–ISBN 978-1-55451-540-0 (pbk.)

1. Basketball—Juvenile poetry. I. Rasmussen, Gerry, 1956-
II. Title.

PS8573E79.C72 2013   jC811'.54   C2013-901051-3

Distributed in Canada by:
Firefly Books Ltd.
50 Staples Ave., Unit 1
Richmond Hill, ON
L4B 0A7

Published in the U.S.A. by:
Annick Press (U.S.) Ltd.
Distributed in the U.S.A. by:
Firefly Books (U.S.) Inc.
P.O. Box 1338, Ellicott Station
Buffalo, NY 14205

The artwork in this book was done in pen and ink and Photoshop.
The poems are set in Chaparall Pro. Titles are in Bryan Talbot Lower,
with page numbers in Shake Open, both from www.comicfonts.com.

Printed in China

Visit us at: www.annickpress.com
Visit the author at: www.lorislesynski.com
        or www.crazyaboutbasketball.ca
Visit the illustrator at: www.gerryrasmussen.com

You can write to Loris
c/o Annick Press, 15 Patricia Avenue, Toronto ON
M2M 1H9 Canada
or e-mail her at
LorisLesynski@gmail.com

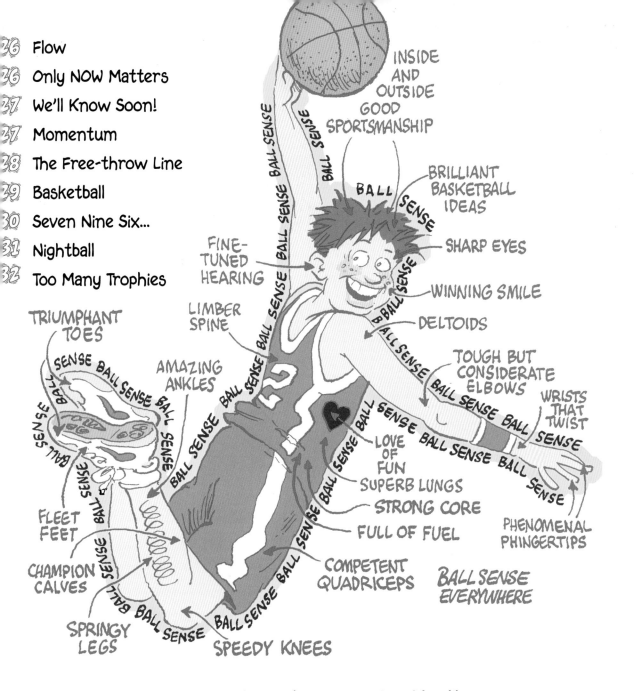

Born to Play Basketball

Your feet just lumps of muscle,
  your arms just sacks of skin,
your eyeballs wobbly jelly blobs
  until the games begin.

Then something brilliant happens—
  all your parts (and in between)
connect and shoot together!
  You're a basketball machine!

Game On!

the center circle's
   where it starts
fans' and players'
   thumping hearts
the game is on!
   the whistle blows!
there's the jump ball
   up it goes!
instantly the ball's
   in play
we're fired up
   to rule today

a great fast break
   the team is pumped
and right away
   the ball is dunked
another pass
   another throw
no one knows
   which way we'll go!
got it! shot it!
   YES, it's in!
our destiny today?
   to win!

another foul!
   again it's time
for nerves of steel
   on the free-throw lin
some lousy shots
   and tragic misses
man oh man,
   a game like this is
too exciting,
   fans are screaming
players grinning
   coach is beaming

eaps and shots
  beyond astounding
ball is bouncing
  feet are pounding
half-time break
  review mistakes
then *in* again
  for all it takes!
we run the floor
  and run it hard
outwitting each
  and every guard

the ref shouts out
  a foul, and then
a free-throw flub!
  behind again
the fans are tense
  suspense is high
the final seconds
  flying by
an outside shot
  goes off the rim
the next one drops
  exactly in

the shot clock stops
  the game is done
we got the point!
  we won? *WE WON!*
the gym is full of
  joy and sweat
(and on the other
  side, regret)
but play or watch,
  such great suspense
and either way
  the thrill's immense!

From the Ball's Point of View

What's the most popular
game of all?

For balls, of course,
it's BASKETBALL.

We don't get clubbed.
We don't get hit.

A free throw doesn't
hurt a bit.

We don't get smacked.
There are no kicks.

We never get attacked
with sticks.

It's always so exciting when

we *bounce*,
then *bounce*,
then *BOUNCE*
again!

And much as we *LIKE*
the pats we get,

boy, do we *LOVE*
getting dunked in the net!

Crazy About Basketball!

the feel of it
appeal of it
the belong of it
in my hand

the size of it
surprise of it
as I plan where it's
gonna land

the game of it
the aim of it
we love it *every time*
I think this year our basketball
should get a valentine!

Basketball = Life

the world is made
of bounce and aim

basketball's
not *just* a game

in every little cell alive,
you'll find a move,
a bounce, a jive

atoms vibrate all the time
in people, puppies,
trees, and slime

a grain of sand
a drop of blood
a gasp of air
a blob of mud

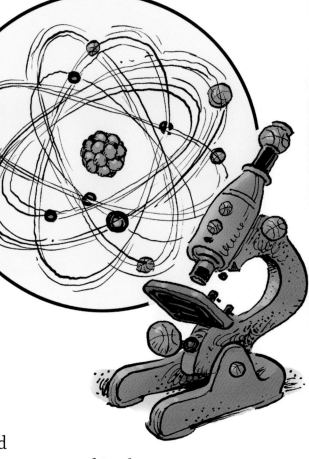

everything has
bounce inside it
even rocks
although they hide it

everything
you'll ever know
is always moving,
on the go

the universe?
this brilliant game?
they sometimes seem
a lot the same

Everything that happens happens when the time is right.

When basketball became a game, it wasn't overnight.

The "simple" things it needed weren't possible before.

First of all, there had to be a flat, enormous floor.

In ancient times, the caves and halls had wide and open spaces,

but stony floors of olden days were rough and bumpy places.

Modern floors were smooth at last,

and *WOW! Electric light!*

Then proper balls were needed to be

"dribbled" left and right.

Balls before were heavy lumps,

or blown-up piggy bladders.

But truly round and bouncing high?

For basketball, it matters.

"Vulcanizing" meant

the air inside was sealed up tight.

Finally—a ball that *really* bounced,

and did it right!

Balls for ancient Aztec games were solid and heavy, weighing as much as six basketballs.

The ball most used in olden days was a blown-up pig bladder, sometimes covered, sometimes not. It bounced quite crookedly, and wore out quickly.

he first basketball was a occer ball—not even lose to perfectly round, nd the thick laces poiled the direction of host bounces.

How Basketball Was Born

A smart and nice professor-coach
   in 1891
knew his students needed
   winter exercise and fun.
But not all sports would fit indoors
   and something new was needed.
He looked around. With what he found,
   he totally succeeded.

Dr. James Naismith
Canadian
1861-1939

No goalpost "wins" in indoor gyms.
   No nets at which to shoot.
Then right outside, he spied
   some sturdy baskets full of fruit.
"For *GOALS? Aha!*" was Dr. Naismith's
   loud inspired shout.
They all agreed—but said, "We better
   take the peaches out!"
Dr. Naismith taught the kids
   the way to play his game.
The students really liked it, making
   "*basket*ball" its name.
They nailed the basket ten feet high
   and threw the ball—but *then*
they had to climb up every time
   to bring it down again!

HMMM.
~~LACROSS~~
~~SOCCE~~
~~BASEB~~

Perhaps one day a player saw
a fisherman and thought
a *net* would be a better way
to capture every shot.
So early hoops and rims went on,
but still they climbed up—
WHAT?

Fifteen years would pass before
they got the bottoms cut!

Bit by bit, the coaches tried out
different rules and terms,
which (for now) are final and
what every player learns.
Does basketball need any more
improvements to the game?
We'll wait and see what happens—
will it change, or stay the same?

Cement, invented later, made
a perfect playground court
and basketball became an *OUT-* as well as *IN-*
door sport.

Dr. Naismith
met his wife
the very day
he went
to watch the
first official
women's basketball
event.

Uniforms Then & Now

In olden days, the coaches chose
for uniforms, such heavy clothes
that players mostly got too hot
to ever really score a lot.

As fashions changed
they got a chance
to give up itchy woollen pants
and very short and shiny shorts
were what was worn
on all the courts.

Then longer shorts became the style
but after just a little while
designers made them longer still
and kept it up for years until
a brand new season now presents
new shorts the size of
circus tents!

Bigger and bigger,
that's the trend.
Wonder where
it's going to end!

How Basketball's Different from Other Sports

nets the smallest
players tallest
ball is fastest
most precise

some sports older
many colder
(those the ones
they play on ice)

no other sport
of any sort
has slam dunks...
dribbles...
H-O-R-S-E

should all the rest
agree it's best?
the answer is
"OF COURSE!"

Hoops on Ice

They say in Lithuania
they have a kind of mania
for basketball on skates, on ice.
A chilly way to train-i-a!

Talk About Crowded!

you always
have to be aware
of who is here
and who is there
of where
they are
how near, how far
*off*ence! *de*fence!
be prepared!
there's someone THERE!

AND *THERE!*

AND *THERE!*

Ball Sense
Your ball sense?
Essential!
You can't play
without it.
Find it,
believe in it,
don't ever
doubt it.

14

"Close" Doesn't Count

A bit of a miss is the same as a lot.
With everyone watching, I botch up the shot.
But wasn't that throw
a magnificent sight?
If only the hoop was
a bit to the right...
OHHHHHHHH
WELLLLLLLL....

Dribble Rhythm

Shoot a lot
and **score** a lot
and **miss** a lot
and **pass** a lot.
Win a lot and
lose a lot
and **play** a lot
all day a lot.
Keep it up!
Take a shot!
Had enough?
Not.

15

NOT in the Shoes

Miss or score?

Win or lose?

It's *never* in

the shoes

you choose!

Don't get confused

by ads, refuse

to let them tell you

you must use

the ones they sell.

(*Buy now! Buy new!*)

At heart you know

what's really true:

the win's in you and

not the shoe.

Everything's a Hoop

The world as seen
by Dunkin' Jim:
everything's a hoop
to him.

No matter what
he's looking at,
he wonders:

Could I aim for that?

Is that a place a ball could go?

is all he ever wants to know.

From what angle?

From how far?

Figures what his
chances are.
In his mind, plays
night and day.
Never puts the ball away.

That Smallest Sound

The footsteps pound.

The high-tops squeak.

The crowd is loud.

The floorboards creak.

But through it all,

we catch the sound,

the one that's high above the ground,

that most important noise of all:

the *swishing* of the basketball.

Doesn't even touch the rim

just *whooooosh*—

y'hear it?

YES, it's in!

TALL

Is tall all

that matters?

Is tall all

that counts?

Can somebody tall

give a ball

better bounce?

Sometimes *yes*.

Sometimes *no*.

Any height's right

once you know

how to throw.

Scientifically Accurate

you *know*

you're *not*

too *tall* or too *short*

if your *feet* reach *the floor*

of the basketball court

Q: What should you call a basketball star?

A: Your highness.

Audience Point of View

every time
we watch them play

it almost takes our
breath away

for even though
we're in the stands

it's like the ball's
between our hands

shooting! passing!

dunking! scoring!

basketball is
NEVER boring

too exciting!
such suspense!

no wonder we're
XTREMELY tense!

What I Want Today

a sweet shot

a sure shot

a beautiful arc

watch

the ball dive

like a great

white shark

Best Floor to Score

It isn't *just* about
the ball,
a bounce that's
high or low.
It matters what it
bounces ON—
that makes it fast
or slow.
A bounce on sand
is useless,
so is grass or any mat.
Playground courts
are bumpy
so you have to deal
with that.
But floors in gyms
are wonderful
(and perfect for
your knees).
So every time you
pass the ball, say,
*"Thank you,
maple trees!"*

21

This is True

Taylor trained her fingertips
   for weeks and weeks and weeks.
Every day she practiced twenty
   fingertip techniques:
rolls and spins and backs and forths
   and power dribbles low,
movements fast and furious,
   preparing for a throw.
      Her hands were fast and sensitive,
         her finger pads like glue,
            but then it seemed
               her arms and legs
                  got better faster, too!

Who knew? *It's true*
   that strengthening
      your fingers on the ball
         makes every other part of you
            get stronger overall.

This Little Piggy...

Finger position *hugely* counts
for every pass and every bounce.
For every throw you have to know
exactly where your fingers go.

Left & Right

My left and right?
I found out these
have different
personalities.
One's a baby,
one's the boss,
each can make
an awesome toss.
So practice means
I change and switch
until I don't know
which is which.
Back and forth
and back I go
and in a while
you'd never know
that one was leader,
one was not.
My hands team up
for every shot!

The Best!

Scientists did
a bouncing test
of balls with air inside
(compressed):
tennis balls, volleyballs,
footballs, the rest.
And of them all
(if you take a guess)
were **basketballs**
the bounciest?
YES!

(But imagine a job
where you never play,
just measure dozens
bounces all day!)

Basketball Fuel

put crummy gas
in an awesome car?
you won't go fast
you won't go far

if, today,
the way i play
is so much worse
than yesterday

it may be what
i ate and drank
what went in
my own gas tank

basketball stars
(it's no surprise)
don't train on candy,
chips, and fries

basketball players,
we gotta repeat:
what we eat
affects our feet

Flow

fake left
  spin right
move fast
  move light
brain on red alert
  in motion
heart is pumping
  with emotion
some moves smooth
some sharp and angled
don't know *how*
  we stay untangled

Only NOW Matters

hours of practic[e]
months of drills
years to learn
the trickiest ski[ll]
all boil down to
right this minut[e]
get in the game
and **win** i[t]

We'll Know Soon!

one team'll be happy
one team'll be sad
one'll feel fabulous
one'll feel bad
one'll be grinning
one drying their eyes
but which will be which?
every game's a surprise!

Momentum
MO
MO
MO MEN TUM!
Get me some!
Get me some!
Strategeeeeeeee!
Energeeeee!
Basketball
technologeeeee!
Mix them up
all fast and loose,
got me my
momentum
juice!

The Free-throw Line

I've missed before
    BUT NOT THIS TIME.
I'm calm and cool at
    the free-throw line.
I bend my knees.
    I clear my mind.
I concentrate. I wait.
    It's time.
I shoot! The hoop is
    MINE, ALL MINE!
      I've figured out
        the free-throw line!

Basketball

in Spanish	in Polish	in Persian	in Finnish
Baloncesto	Koszykówka	بازی بسکتبال	Koripallo

in Icelandic	in Chinese	in Portuguese	in Turkish
Körfubolti	篮球	Basquetebol	Basketbol

Around the world *buh-BOMP, buh-BOMP*

  in Canada, Italy, Denmark, Japan,

game after game is going on,

  buh-BOMP, buh-BOMP in every land.

Buh-BOMP in Australia, *buh-BOMP* in Peru,

  in China, Aruba, in Fiji, too.

Greece *buh-BOMP* and the U.S.A.

  Buh-BOMP all the kids in Jamaica play.

Malta, Gibraltar, *buh-BOMP* Brazil,

  different languages, similar drill.

In India, Germany, Sweden, and Guam,

  buh-BOMP a ball for every palm.

In every country, every minute,

  someone's dribbling *somewhere* in it.

Buh-BOMP, buh-BOMP the world's become

  buh-BOMP, buh-BOMP a basketball drum.

29

Seven Nine Six...

(THIS IS THE SHELF WHERE
AUTOBIOGRAPHIES AND
OTHER BASKETBALL BOOKS
ARE FOUND IN ANY LIBRARY)

When pros write an
autobiography,
they're talking to me,
they're talking to me.

They write about how
they decided to play.
No one was great
from the very first day.

They tell me the troubles
they had as a kid
and some of the sillier things
they did.

They put into words
how they mastered the game.
They write what it's like
having fortune and fame.

Their stories are great,
just like watching them play.

(Someone might read
about *me*
some day!)

Nightball

can't go in
  I know it's night
but have to get my
  shooting right

playground's empty
  dark and cold
but here I'll stay
  until I'm old
if that's how long it takes
  to get
the hang of landing in
  the net

streetlight shows
  a perfect arc
the *swish* sounds louder
  in the dark
a lot of shots, a little spin,
  and some still miss
—but more get in!

bet I'm better
  really soon
my biggest fan tonight?
  the moon

Too Many Trophies

There are trophies
on the benches.
There are trophies
on the floor.
There are trophies in
the lockers, there's
no room for any more.
It isn't that we
always win
(that's only in our dreams)—
selling discount trophies
is the way
we fund the team.

Want *more* basketball poems? Write some of your own!
Find out how at www.crazyaboutbasketball.ca